Today I Am...

DISCOVER YOUR INNER WORLD

Today I Am...

CARMEN WARRINGTON

hachette
AUSTRALIA

hachette
AUSTRALIA

This edition published in Australia and New Zealand in 2017
by Hachette Australia
(an imprint of Hachette Australia Pty Limited)
Level 17, 207 Kent Street, Sydney NSW 2000
www.hachette.com.au

First published as *Who Am I?* in 2004 by Thomas C. Lothian Pty Limited

10 9 8 7 6 5 4 3 2 1

National Library of Australia
Cataloguing-in-Publication data:

Warrington, Carmen, author.
Today I am.../Carmen Warrington.

ISBN 978 0 7336 3653 0 (paperback)

Peace of mind.
Contentment.
Affirmations.
Self-help techniques.

158.1

Cover design by Hannah Janzen
Cover image courtesy of iStock
Internal design by Kirby Jones
Internal images courtesy of Shutterstock
Typeset in Helvetica Neue Light by Kirby Jones
Printed and bound in Great Britain by Clays Ltd, St Ives plc

acknowledgements

I have been fortunate to meet hundreds of inspiring people; thank you all for sharing your discoveries and realisations with me, and for shaping my thinking. I express my deep thanks to: the BKs for teaching me to meditate and for guiding me on my journey towards love and light; my mother and father, my sister Lisa, and my brother Jan, for nurturing my creative spirit, and teaching me so many virtues; and all my fantastic friends who enthusiastically supported this book, and who have always believed in me.

Thanks also to Magnolia Flora for first publishing this book under the title *Who Am I?* and to Sophie Hamley for breathing new life into this edition.

My eternal thanks to David for his loving kindness. And my unending gratitude to the Source of All Inspiration.

introduction

We all play roles in life: daughter, son, mother, father, partner, friend, sister, brother. There are other roles we play, depending on the situation and the people we are with. These roles are aspects of ourselves but they're not really who we are.

Over time, the roles we play can become who we are. They can take over the true essence of our soul until we don't know what is deep inside us. At those times, we feel disconnected from our real self. We also feel how important it is to reconnect, although we might not know how to do this.

Today I Am… offers you the opportunity to explore the richness of your inner world in all its colours, shades and contrasts. Open any page on any day and contemplate the soul sketch that is there: you may be a feather, you may be a balloon, you may be an earthquake.

Carry this contemplation with you throughout the day, week, month – however long you wish, and then choose another.

By exploring these different aspects of your nature, you will come to know yourself more deeply – and to know yourself is the greatest secret of all.

today
I am...

a peace
dove

I am a messenger of peace. I don't convey my message through words, for the olive branch I carry would fall from my beak.

It is not through my actions that I convey my peace message, though I never use my wings to attack. My wings are for flight. From high above the Earth I can see that national boundaries do not really exist. Nothing truly separates one human being from another, and from my vantage point I can only marvel at the wonder of every living thing.

The respect I have for all life is the message of peace I bring.

today
I am...

spring

This is my time of new birth and new growth. Suddenly one day there is a feeling of vitality in the air, and everything awakens after a deep, nourishing sleep. It is a time of rapid growth, the blossoming of creative forces in full flight. My energy is fresh and exuberant. It is the time of excitement, wonder and optimism.

But if spring was eternal, with constant growth, I would become depleted of energy, exhausted. After new growth I need to sustain and develop what I have created. Slowly but surely, the cycle turns.

today
I am...

a traveller

I am on a one-way journey. I left the starting point long ago and there's no turning back. My destination lies ahead, but to focus solely on the journey's end is to miss the gifts I am offered each step of the way. I have many travelling companions who stay with me until their own journey steers them on a different course — then we part company.

Whenever I face a major crossroad or obstacle, my guide is there to offer counsel. The path I take is dictated by my own choices, so my guide remains silent until I seek advice.

today
I am...

a bird in flight

I was born with the gift of faith. My birthright is to soar high above the world. I can steer a course with the wind and enjoy the freedom of flight. I fly in harmony with my flock or experience the joyous solitude of my own company.

Desiring to be in the celestial blue, all I need do is leave my tree and fly, but sometimes doubts and fears keep me clinging to its branches. I have faith in the wind. I reaffirm my faith in myself and let go.

today I am...

an actor

In my lifelong career I play a variety of roles, many within a single day. Each role I assume requires a set of behaviours: a leader exercises authority, a team member co-operates, a parent nurtures and guides, a counsellor listens intently, an agent for change challenges the way things are.

An actor's mastery lies in removing the previous role before beginning the next. The danger in being an actor is that I can lose myself in a role, and believe that I am the role I play.

At the end of the day I remove all the trappings of the characters I have portrayed and come back to my essential self.

today
I am...

a buried treasure

I contain riches beyond belief. I am rich in qualities, virtues, traits and talents, gifts that were inherited at birth and to which I have added value over a lifetime of experiences. Yet somehow the wealth within me remains hidden, and I believe that I am only worthless rocks and pebbles.

I have acquired many beliefs about myself from my society and my family. These beliefs might not have been imposed intentionally, but they weigh me down. I loosen the compacted soil of others' beliefs, bringing my treasure to the surface.

today I am...

a mountain stream

My journey begins high in the mountain peaks, where the atmosphere is pure, unpolluted by the trappings of daily life. Purity is my essence. My purpose is movement, and the downward slope entices me on an adventure to the ocean. Along the way I gather momentum and strength. Along the way I accumulate impurities, but I am not the rubbish I carry. Once I reach my destination I will release all impurities into the vast, purifying waters.

Recalling my sweet, clean essence, I filter out all the waste, all the negativity I have accumulated, and I experience my purity.

today
I am...

an infant

I have a great passion to learn, and failure is an incentive for me to try again. I make progress through enthusiastic trial and error. Learning to walk is an adventure. I often fall, but I get up and try again and eventually succeed. And once I have mastered walking, I want to run!

I remain enthusiastic. I keep trying regardless of setbacks, not wanting to give up. I encourage myself: 'Keep going. Never mind if you fall, get up and try again. You can do it. We all make mistakes. You're doing well.'

today
I am...

a jewel

A jewel has no desire to be set in silver or gold, to be made into a necklace or a ring. The jewel is content no matter how the jeweller chooses to fashion its housing.

Even if I am hidden away in a drawer I know my own worth, my own beauty. My radiance remains constant. I don't need to be noticed to know my true value. In a world that reveres the illusion of fame and celebrity, I practise the art of self-appreciation. I am content with who I am, with what I have. I am content with my life.

today
I am...

a student

I am a student in the school of life, taking a practical course in happiness. People, situations and events present me with opportunities for learning. Instead of asking 'Why me?' the student asks 'What is the lesson here?' I am in a class of my own, a class especially made for me. Until a lesson is learnt its circumstances will continue to recur, in a variety of shapes and forms. I may be given small tests or a major examination to chart my progress in the school of life.

To pass with honour, I work closely with my wise teacher, who encourages me to discover my own answers. In this way I gain lasting wisdom.

today
I am...

a warrior

I am a brave warrior. My task is simple: I must face the enemy with courage. I keep facing my enemies, never turning my back to run away. My enemies are the things that rob me of my peace and power. I know beyond doubt that no matter what the situation, no matter what the challenge, my enemy is within me. The enemy is not anything or anyone else, the enemy is my own weakness, my own shortcomings.

For every weakness in me I have an opposing strength. In facing my enemies I come to know which weapons will bring me victory.

today
I am...

an open palm

I accept everything that life offers me. No opportunity is missed. I am able to receive the next gift because I have let go of the previous one.

Sometimes I hold on too tightly, afraid that no more gifts will come my way. By holding on I block other possibilities and I risk crushing what I hold so tightly in my clenched fist.

I allow all things to come and go, and cherish them while they are in my safekeeping.

today I am...

a guest

Being the guest, I am carefree. This is not my residence, and everything I use is a gift from my host. I am grateful for all that I receive. I appreciate even the smallest gestures of kindness, the simplest offerings. Nothing is taken for granted. Gratitude comes easily for a guest who is bestowed with many blessings while simply passing through life.

today I am...

a moonless night

There is no light in my dark sky. The way ahead is obscured and I relish the blackness. It is all I have and it consumes me.

The darkness and I become one. All that is dark in me arises: it longs to be known yet cannot abide the light, concealing itself in the presence of the moon. Sometimes, terrifying monsters emerge that I never knew were within me. They linger and prowl and make themselves known to me.

Touched by the new moon's first light, the darkness vanishes, but I have felt it. Now that I recognise what lies within me, I can begin another cycle of self-transformation.

today
I am...

summer

This is my time of abundance. Success comes easily as I enjoy the flowers and fruits of my earlier labours. This is a time of fullness and expansion as I nurture and develop my new creations to their full potential. Youthful energy ripens into maturity.

But if summer was eternal, expansion would reach its limits and boredom or inertia would set in. After fullness, I desire to make some changes. Slowly but surely, the cycle turns.

today
I am...

a rechargeable
battery

I am powerful, but my energy supply has limits:
when I use it, I lose it. I am wise about what
drains my energy and what empowers me. I can
recharge easily, and how I recharge depends
on what type of energy I want to replace.
Physical energy requires physical replenishment,
spiritual energy requires spiritual topping up.

An unlimited power source is always available to me.
Whenever I want, I can plug into the source and fill
my soul with as much power as I want.

today
I am...

a reporter

I have a passion for passing on what I see, hear or witness, but I never pass on what I witness without adding my own opinions. I shape the story to suit my purpose, and I am selective about what I report. I construct the story I want to tell by including and excluding certain pieces of information.

The question is, 'What is my purpose in reporting?' Is it to uplift or to stir up unrest? Or is my purpose to spread peace and goodwill? An important question I ask myself before I launch into my next report is, 'Why am I telling this story?'

today
I am...

the sea

When the weather is calm my waves roll gently. When stormy winds blow I am wild and out of control. On the surface I am influenced by my surroundings. But I am also deep, and way down beneath my surface is another world. In my depths I have a mysterious and secret world of stillness, silence, beauty, hidden colour and great power.

Instead of dwelling on the surface where I interact with the world outside, I spend time visiting my depths so that I can become resilient to the winds of change.

today I am...

an instrument

The virtuoso musician makes beautiful music through me. The musician has unlimited creative power, but I am the means to express that well of creativity. Without me, the musician has only talent, but the marriage of player and instrument creates music. What music will be played through me today, and who shall accept the applause?

today I am...
autumn

This is my time of reflection and release, for gathering and giving away. A cool change inspires me to harvest my creations and store for the future. What is unused decays, and what is not relevant is released. Change is in the air and I let go of what was, making way for what will be.

But if autumn was eternal, the sense of loss would be overwhelming; I might let go too much and be left with nothing. I need to make new plans and to create new dreams. Slowly but surely the cycle turns.

today I am...

a caretaker

I came naked into this world, and when I leave I will take nothing with me, not even the body I call my own.

I have accumulated many objects around me. I have journeyed with many people. I do not own anything or anyone, not even my children. As a caretaker my duty is to care for that which is placed in my trust. I enjoy the things in my life, but my enjoyment does not depend on those things. To claim ownership is to be trapped in the material world, where I will be consumed by desires and suffer many hurts and disappointments. So I remain a simple caretaker.

today
I am...

a stick of
incense

Mysterious, other-worldly wafts of smoke curl through the air, circling, dreamily rising. I am releasing the smoke of my thoughts, my attitudes, my intentions, my feelings. Although these are subtle, they do have an effect. They permeate the atmosphere and influence the mood in the room.

If my thoughts are negative, my attitude less than generous and my intention destructive, I release a heavy, pungent odour. If my thoughts are kind, my attitude understanding and my intention to bring about benefit, my fragrant aroma uplifts the atmosphere.

I influence the atmosphere in subtle yet powerful ways.

today
I am...

a star

I've been put up here to be.

Not to do — to be.

Up here I am way beyond the cares and troubles of the world — I am free just to be. Free to radiate light, for my essence is light and peace. Anyone who looks up at the night sky can feel my peace. I am blissfully detached up here, removed from everything and everyone, but when I want to I can shoot down to earth, straight back to activity. I love the simplicity up here; the peace. Occasionally, it's good for the soul just to be.

today
I am...

a diamond

I was once coal; black carbon buried deep underground. In the dark I have endured intense heat and borne incredible pressure. I have endured, and my endurance of pressure and heat has rearranged my molecules into the perfect structure of the diamond.

Now I am a jewel of great beauty, but I am not fragile or delicate. Thanks to the pressures I have learnt to tolerate, I am tough and resilient and can withstand many things without harming my essential beauty. My energy is not distracted by life's pressures, so I am free to play with the light.

today I am...

a raindrop

Compared to the ocean, a single raindrop seems insignificant, ridiculously small and inconsequential. But in the thirsty desert, a single raindrop is precious, life-giving and vitally important. To give something when and where it is needed is what really counts. Then it is a truly valued gift.

Is our world an ocean of peace or a desert? Even though I am only a single drop, every drop of peace counts. I do make a difference.

today
I am...

the moon

I run playful circles around the Earth, but I have a love affair with the Sun. The Earth is the world with which I interact, for it is where my light falls, but the Sun is the source of my light. I play a game with the Sun, orbiting the playing field of Earth, while keeping my face to the Sun.

The dance of life takes the three of us into many configurations. Sometimes the Earth stands between me and my beloved Sun and I fall into darkness. Sometimes I am completely bathed in sunlight and the Earth enjoys my radiant fullness. What a dance! What a game of waxing and waning light! What bliss when I am fully facing the Sun.

today
I am...

a mountain
climber

Exhilaration fills my lungs as I make my way up the slope, fuelled by the prospect of attaining the peak. Conditions are harsh and the weather conspires against me. As the difficulties mount, the small voice that was urging me to turn back yells in my face, 'Give up!' But the dream won't go away and my determination increases. I discover the meaning of perseverance as I push myself higher, until finally I am at the top. I've done it. The view from up here is intoxicating.

In the distance a higher peak captures my imagination; before the descent is over I am dreaming again.

today
I am...

a jewel-trader

I deal in precious gems; I don't waste my time with worthless rocks. I have learnt to tell the difference, sometimes the hard way. People cheated me, and I took their fakes in good faith. Each mistake honed my eye, sharpened my wits, and refined my ability to discern what is of value. I trust more and more in my intuition, and can sense what is true and what is false.

today
I am...

a pendulum

I seek balance, always. In my quest I swing from one side to the other, sometimes wildly, and seemingly out of control. I must explore both extremes and all points in between or I will be pulled later to what I have not already investigated.

The still centre, which I crave, is the result of visiting all possibilities, all extremes.

today I am...

a butterfly

At present I am in my cocoon, but I was born to be a butterfly. With time and the nurturing warmth of the sun, I will fulfil my destiny. For now I dream of my true colours. I dream of flight and of a beautiful field of flowers in which I will dance. Transformation is inevitable. In fact, transformation is underway. I focus on my beautiful future; my patience will be rewarded.

today I am...

an elastic band

When nothing is bothering me, I am relaxed. Then something comes along and gets under my skin. I hook onto it and it pulls me out of my peaceful state. It tugs me, it pulls me, it stretches me to the point of tension, until I think I will break.

All I have to do is let it go with my mind. It is not holding onto me, I am holding onto it. If I don't hold onto it anymore, I will instantly snap back to my former shape.

today
I am...

a cloud

My life revolves around giving, but it never feels like a burden. I relax. I float in the sky. I am light and easy. I have no need to rush, no need to do anything.

When I have rested, the sun coaxes me to gather water from the ocean and fill myself with life-giving droplets of rain. I fill myself up before I give to others. This is a kind of self-service. When I am a full rain cloud, I shower my contents onto the thirsty earth.

today I am...

a balloon

I was born to celebrate. I am a reminder that an ordinary event can be a celebration of life. I am filled with the breath of happiness. I am light and joyful and buoyant.

My happiness has nothing to do with the world outside. Nothing outside me can destroy my happiness. If my happiness diminishes it is because the air is leaking out of me. I attend to my weaknesses and repair any holes so that my happiness remains intact.

today
I am...

a superhero

I am fulfilled when I can be of service to humanity.
I have a special ability that was given to me at birth.
Sometimes it takes all my ingenuity to work out how
my power will help in a particular situation.

Sometimes I forget that I am a superhero and
believe I am just an ordinary mortal. At these times it
is impossible to access my superpower. To use my
power I simply remember who I am and what I have
to offer the world.

today I am...

a magnet

Who I believe I am has a more powerful influence over me than who I am. Each belief I hold carries a magnetic field that draws a similar energy towards me. The more conviction I have that a belief is true, the more powerful is its magnetic pull.

If I believe I am lucky, good fortune is attracted to me. If I believe I deserve to be treated badly, I attract abusive relationships. If I believe I am nothing special, I attract experiences in which I become invisible. My worst fears and my greatest hopes are magnetically attracting experiences to me. It is time to review the beliefs I hold about myself.

today
I am...

a garden

I am full of life, beautiful life. I flourish and grow through many seasons, enjoying ever-changing blazes of colour and shape in buds, blossoms, flowers, berries, leaves, trees and grasses. I give great joy and pleasure to the gardener.

Of course, I have some weeds. I am a garden, and every living thing finds expression in me. I feel no shame about my weeds. They are natural, and the gardener will tend to them when the time is right, for timing is an important aspect of the gardener's work. I am proud of who I am. If I only see my weeds, I cannot appreciate the beauty of all my luxurious flowers and shrubs, or the majesty of each tree.

today I am...

a block of ice

I am brittle, static and unyielding. Something triggered a painful reaction in me and the only way I could cope was to shut down. My ability to love has frozen over. Bitter cold winds blow across my words and people slip and slide on my frosty intentions. I am icy cold and uninviting.

Fortunately, this state is not permanent and a simple remedy exists. I apply warmth. I will melt, and love will flow again. If I start to warm from inside me, my heart will thaw more quickly.

today I am...

a bushfire

An incident set off a spark, a reaction in me that ignited my anger. How small was that spark and how all-consuming and out of control is the fire that blazes now.

The truth is that the land was dry, the trees were parched, primed for another fire to flare. The terrain was still smoking, the embers still smouldering from an earlier outburst.

I am on the rampage now, devouring everything in my path; but while I am consumed with fury I can't stop the inferno. I will have deep regrets later, but my passionate outburst is unstoppable. People are avoiding me — they don't want to get burnt. If only the rain would come. Cool reason will save me. Understanding will moisten the land and prevent this destructive rage from re-igniting.

today
I am...

an earthquake

Down in the core of my being, major shifts are taking place. I am redefining myself at the deepest level and nothing will ever be the same again. When the foundation rearranges itself, everything built upon it becomes unstable. Up on the surface, there is upheaval of catastrophic proportions. Life is completely disrupted, alarms are sounding and damage control is the only way ahead until the shaking stops.

The quaking ground frightens people, but I could not go on as things were. My deeply suppressed needs are surfacing and must be dealt with. As I learn to respond to my needs rather than burying them, the frequency of these massive disruptions will decrease.

today
I am...

a lake

I am shapeless water. My nature is fluid; I adapt according to my needs. Whatever my surroundings are, I take on their shape. My way is not to resist but to surrender to the circumstances of the moment. I do not force things to be the way I want them to be, but go with the flow. This is the source of my serenity. In surrendering to the way things are I find stillness. Freed from upheaval and resistance, I am at peace.

today
I am...

a rock

I am solid rock. My nature is enduring; I stay true to myself no matter what changes occur around me. I protect the way things are. I am not seduced by novelty. I respect the past and won't abandon it without good reason.

I am strong and resistant, but not stubborn. I can be moulded. Over time I can be shaped by water. Patience is my great virtue, the secret to my inner peace.

today
I am...

an alchemist

I have mastered the art of transforming something worthless into something priceless. I can turn lead into gold.

The artistry of transformation is in my perception. The secret is to see the innate value of everything. Respect things for what they are and they become gold.

The same applies to people. Each person on this Earth is part of God's creation, and who am I to doubt their worth? The alchemy is to focus on the pure gold within each one. This takes great determination, but my pure heart and my divine vision are strong enough to overlook the visible lead and seek the hidden gold.

today
I am...

a bridge-builder

Once there was a single land, but now there are many isolated islands, surrounded by the waters of my tears. I separated myself from people with whom I shared toxic relationships in the past.

To recover my sense of wholeness and wellbeing, I choose to make links between the islands. Not for those people to re-enter my life, but for me to revisit my past with wisdom and understanding. I own my part in allowing, accepting and prolonging their poisonous behaviour. I own any unfair expectations I placed upon them. I open my heart and forgive. I build bridges to heal the rifts in my soul.

today I am...

an hourglass

The master of time has filled my upper chamber with sand; until every grain has trickled into the lower chamber I must be patient. Nothing can hurry or interfere with divine timing.

Each task, each project, each lesson, each process is subject to divine timing. I am learning to live fully in the present as I contemplate each grain passing through the narrow neck and into its place below. The grains fall second by second, moment by moment.

today I am...

a feather

The winds of destiny summon me to my future and my journey continues. I float blissfully along on gentle breezes and upward-spiralling currents of warm air. Sometimes a strong gust catches me unaware, propelling me into the unknown. At other times I lie inert where I have been dumped by violent, battering winds.

A feather has no power to resist the force of the winds. I must simply remain light so that my landing will be painless. My lightness of being allows me to catch hold of even a slight puff of wind, so that I can follow my destiny.

today
I am...

a rose bush

My talent is to bloom with perfumed flowers. I give immense pleasure to anyone who chances upon my exquisite roses. My thorns are equally renowned. They are my defence. If I am frightened because someone is getting too close, my thorns pierce their tender skin and they recoil from me.

But not everyone who approaches me will hurt me. Most people just want to come close to my flowers and enjoy their lovely fragrance. Sharing my gifts is good for both of us. With courage I learn to trust and to communicate my needs.

today
I am...

a sparrow

I am a humble creature with no particular claim to fame. I am not powerful like the eagle, colourful like the parrot or majestic like the peacock. I am small and plain, indistinguishable from other sparrows.

Yet every morning I announce the dawn. And I don't just whisper, I sing my heart out. Although it's possible that not a single creature will hear my song, I simply use the talents I was given.

My strength lies in my self-worth. I'm happy with who I am. I don't long to swap places with the eagle, the parrot or the peacock. And I am fortunate: I am the first creature kissed by the rays of the sun each morning.

today
I am...

a storm

My thunderous words and flashes of lightning are intended to hurt, but my aim is poor because of all the tears I rain down, so no real harm is done. My tears tell the truth of my stormy outburst — I am hurting inside.

I retreat to my calm centre. It's called the eye of the storm because this is where I look at myself to discover what the turmoil is about. The storm has been brewing for a while. Why did I let it build to this intensity? What am I really feeling? What am I expecting? What have I not communicated?

The damage report is substantial, but at least the air is clear and the atmosphere is not so heavy.

today
I am...

an artist

I express things creatively, the way I see them. If a dozen artists paint the same scene, there will be a dozen different images. How can I say that one version is right or wrong, better or worse than another? Surely it's all a matter of perception.

I see things from a certain angle, with a particular focus. I compose my picture according to my tastes, my intentions. I imbue with meaning and significance all the objects, characters and events that I depict. More importantly, I appreciate that we are all artists, each enjoying our own perspective on life. I honour your perceptions as much as my own.

today
I am...

a tree

I extend my branches in a joyful gesture, celebrating life. What a vibrant and diverse existence this is. I bear the branches of work, family, friends, health, dreams, ambitions. Each branch divides into limbs and twigs; the expansion is astonishing. My life-force pulses through each branch to every single leaf.

And to think I was once just a tiny seed.

When I am overwhelmed by it all, when I wonder how I send my energy to each twig and leaf, I remember the seed. When I concentrate on my essence, I am revitalised.

today I am...

a puppet-master

I acquired this exquisite living puppet a long time ago, and practised for years to bring it completely under my control. Now I carry out complex actions with great artistry, as if the puppet and I are one. It obeys my will and responds to my subtlest intentions.

But I am not the puppet. There is a story to be enacted, written in the pages of destiny. The mastery lies in being unaffected by that story, simply remaining an observer as the drama unfolds, without losing myself in strong emotions. I remain the master and I do not take things personally.

today I am...

a fence

I mark definite boundaries, so people know how far they can go. It's up to me to decide what is private and what is public property. These boundaries can change according to the circumstances; it is my responsibility to ensure that they are clearly defined.

But a fence is not a brick wall, and there are many gates dotted along the perimeter. If you seek my permission, then you may be welcome to enter. However, I reserve the right to say no. All I ask is that you respect my boundaries.

today
I am...

an archer

My thoughts are arrows, and every arrow I release reaches its target. Once an arrow is shot, it cannot be recalled.

Sometimes I play the part of Cupid and my loving thoughts arrive as blessings to the receiver. Sometimes I am a warrior and I mean to wound the enemy. The most dangerous thoughts are those that reach their target on poison-tipped arrows. These are the poisonous thoughts of jealousy, rage, bitterness, resentment and hatred. The poisonous thoughts are doubly damaging for they affect the sender as much as the receiver. To avoid injuring myself I remain aware of the quality of my thoughts.

today I am...

winter

This is my time of withdrawal and recovery. I rest deeply and regenerate. I survive underground with what I have stored and save my energy for introspection. I think, reflect, question. I put things in perspective. I seek new directions and sow the seeds of new ideas. This is the season of gestation, between conception and birth, and nothing is apparent yet.

But if winter was eternal, the unfulfilled potential of new seeds would be unbearable. Life must go on; slowly but surely the cycle turns.

today I am...

a driver

This body is a luxury vehicle that I drive, and all the sense organs are designed to give me maximum pleasure as I travel.

Apart from refuelling, I need to attend to ongoing maintenance. If I don't fix little problems, one day I'll have to take the car off the road for major repairs.

Sometimes my mind is preoccupied and I drive on automatic pilot. That's when habit takes over and I end up in the wrong place. Or accidents occur as I say things I didn't intend, crashing into others' feelings. While driving, I must remain fully conscious, fully aware.

today
I am...

a sunset

Only a certain amount can be achieved in a single
day. I am a reminder that patience is needed,
and that taking a break is a necessary part of any
process. Putting things to rest graciously, I celebrate
with a splendid show of light. I honour the day's
end and mark the passing of that day into history.
The past is now past. I celebrate every single day,
not just the days when a great success is achieved.
I honour the fact that every day is a victory. I shine
light onto all the events of the day, and I find much to
be grateful for.

today
I am...

a scientist

My special research is to discover all about myself and find out how I function best. My method is scientific; it begins with impartial observation. I remain detached from the findings, a mere observer. I study my outward behaviour and its results.

Under the microscope of my awareness I study the subtle energies of my thoughts and feelings. From my observations I formulate theories, which I test through experimentation. If I think like this, how will it make me feel? What will the outcome be? What if I make a subtle change? In this way I become an expert in my subject — the self.

today
I am...

a knight

I am the Lord of my castle, and no one shall conquer me. I have built myself an impenetrable fortress of protection, surrounded by a moat. The drawbridge to my castle will open only when I give the command. I've encased myself in a suit of armour — nobody can hurt me now. It's a shame I'm so hard to embrace with these metal limbs.

I am safe, but at what cost? Is it just the enemy I am keeping out?

today
I am...

a lotus

I am celebrated for my pure white petals and radiant beauty. People think I have a blessed and fortunate existence, floating on the surface of the water having nothing to do with the gritty realities of life in the dirt. Perhaps they don't realise my feet are firmly rooted in the slimy mud. I am well and truly grounded in this earthly plane.

What keeps me above it all? It's not the water; I don't rely on my surroundings to hold me up. What keeps me afloat is the peace of mind I receive from breathing the clean, pure air, and the power I receive from the light of the sun.

today
I am...

a blank page

My story has been written up to this page — the present moment. The main characters have entered; events have unfolded; themes have been introduced and developed. All this influences the next page in my story.

A blank page is powerful because its potential is truly unlimited. Anything can happen now. My story could take a twist and a whole new chapter might begin. The past, although imprinted deeply in the previous pages, has truly passed. This blank page offers freedom from the way things have been. Where will I take my story now?

today I am...

a spider

I weave a wonderful web for myself, drawing all the threads of my life together as one. I move freely around the web, tending to the different aspects of my world.

When I feel needy, insecure or unsure of myself my web becomes sticky, binding everything tightly. My web of attachments traps everything including myself, weighing down my world. One day the web I've spun could collapse under the strain.

I engage in a healthy interaction with the world without becoming trapped. I free myself from attachment to many things: places, possessions, people, opinions; the way I like things done; the way things once were and the way they ought to be. My freedom enables me to fill my world with love.

today
I am...

a snowflake

I am made of the same chemistry as all other snowflakes, but I am shaped by my particular journey through the elements, which gives me a unique identity.

Each snowflake is as beautiful as it is individual. There is no arrogance in my beauty and individuality; it is the wonder of nature. No snowflake is better than another — we are without competition. But each snowflake is more beautiful than the one before.

today I am...

a loudspeaker

I have no on-off switch; I am on continuous broadcast. Whatever is going on inside me is transmitting loud and clear into the immediate environment.

My soul is being projected into the external world. The words I say are just sounds. The actions I perform are simply movement. The real messages coming through the loudspeaker are my thoughts, feelings and intentions. I pay attention to my inner world, doing everything I can to sweeten the music of my soul.

today I am...

a sunrise

The dark night — the domain of dreams and inertia — is over. I herald the new day, where dreams are fulfilled. I offer unlimited opportunities for experiencing love, peace and happiness. A new day is dawning, and it's going to be wonderful. Nothing need ever be the same again. My rosy pink optimism dispels the darkness and my golden enthusiasm invites the sky to display its vast spaciousness where anything is possible. With such a spectacular start, it's going to be a beautiful day.

today I am...

an ecosystem

My natural instinct is to survive; my ability to adapt enables me to do so. I respond and adjust to the many changes that occur in me, both internally and externally.

Above my instinct for survival, I have the will to thrive and flourish. For this I need to maintain the good health of my entire system. All of my parts, the sub-systems that make up my whole, depend upon the proper functioning of my other parts. It's a delicate balance. Each system must be given attention and energy in order that the whole flourishes. If even one system is not healthy it will undermine the wellbeing of the whole.

today
I am...

a tortoise

What a speedy world. It's exhilarating, but oh, the mad acceleration of it all! If I had to go any faster, I think I might expire. I can only do so much. But what I do, I do well and with great concentration, one thing at a time.

Here's how I cope with all the demands on me. Whenever things are getting on top of me, I stop what I am doing and withdraw into my shell. Here I centre myself and remember my natural pace. This keeps me sane, and when I am refreshed I go back into the day.

today I am...

a chameleon

I am very responsive to what is going on around me and I am coloured by the company I keep. My talent is to blend and harmonise with whatever and whomever I am near. I love mingling with other energies and letting them bring out all the varying shades of my personality. It's a great joy for me to express all the different colours of my being. And what are my true colours? All of them are me.

today I am...

a dragon

I am a powerful and formidable creature, a watchful guardian of one of the world's greatest treasures. The treasure chest I guard so closely contains my self-worth.

My wings carry me above any insults hurled my way. Insults, put-downs and abusive words are dispersed by the beating of my wings.

And the fire that I breathe? The fire is for burning any self-destructive words coming from my own mouth.

today I am...

a caged lion

I used to roam the wilderness and knew no fear. But I allowed myself to be trapped in a cage of limitations. I prowl the cage, frightening onlookers with my pent-up frustration. Otherwise I mope around depressed and in a daze. How did I get caught? Perhaps I walked in freely, lured by the promise of an easy life?

I dream of running wild under the open sky. I still sense my potential for a free and magnificent life. I reassess my options: comfort or adventure; predictability or newness; familiarity or exhilaration? When I am ready to step out of the cage I will find that the door was never locked.

today
I am...

an athlete

My goal is to maintain peak performance and to reach my personal best. The only person I am competing with is me. I keep my sights clearly on my goal and go for it. There are some things I can't do, or can't have, but when I focus on my goal, these things do not concern me.

There is no room for doubt — visualising myself as successful is the key. Setbacks, off-days and disappointments are all stepping stones to my success.

today I am...

a movie star

In the story of my life I play the lead role. I have roles in many other stories as well as the one in which I star. In some stories I play a supporting role; in others I am one of the extras.

Not every scene is about me. When it is someone else's scene, I try not to draw the focus towards myself. I keep my opinions in check — this is their scene and they are playing it their own way.

If invited, I give my opinion. Otherwise I refrain from adding to the mass of opinions already out there, even in thought. This leaves me free to concentrate on what I am doing.

today
I am...

a filter

I keep wasteful and harmful impurities from entering the terrain of my mind. It's a huge undertaking: input comes at me from all directions — from my own subconscious, from other people, and incessantly from the media.

Some impurities are subtle and slip through without me noticing them. Frequently I am misinformed about the effect of particular types of thoughts. I mistakenly let these thoughts through because I don't understand their impact on me. After a build-up of these negative thoughts the damage becomes apparent; I become more diligent about what I allow to filter into my mind.

today
I am...

a passenger

My boat is making its way to the opposite shore under the expert handling of the boatman. I sit back, relax, and enjoy the ride. But the passage is not always smooth. When rough waters rock the boat I panic and try to take control, and in the attempt I risk capsizing the vessel. The wisest course of action is to remain calm and trust the boatman to take me safely across the waters. I am in good hands.

today
I am...

a swan

People say I am special: beautiful, noble and graceful. Really, I'm no more special than any other being.

Beautiful? I could complain that I'm too big, my neck is ridiculously long and my feathers are plain white. Graceful? I move through the water with ease, but my wings have been clipped and I can't fly.

In fact, I am special because without any arrogance I choose to see my virtues, not my shortcomings. I'm admired because I accept myself and enjoy the grace and beauty of who I am.

today
I am...

a projector

I consciously project an image of myself that I want the world to see. At the same time I unconsciously project an image of the real me. The result is a blurry double-image, and people can't quite make out who I am. They are confused by the two versions superimposed upon each other.

When I am honest and reveal my true self, when I am the same inside and out, my image comes sharply into focus. Then I can be seen clearly, and my relationships are far more real and beautiful.

today I am...

a torchbearer

I can shine my light or allow the darkness to remain. It's a simple choice — on or off. In the light I see what is real, in the darkness imagination and fear take over. Fear causes me to view your actions with suspicion and think the worst of you.

Then I curse you with harsh judgements and critical opinions. I could bless you back into the light with my good wishes and pure feelings — no matter what you have done. Shall I plunge us both into darkness or into the light? The choice is mine and it's all in the flick of a switch.

today
I am...

a pearl

I was born of mere sand, yet I have a lustre that is highly prized. Without the intense chafing of that single grain of sand I would not be a pearl. The practice of dealing with constant irritations has created layer upon layer of my pearly beauty. There's benefit in everything.

Irritants will always be around, but what will I make of them? Will they remain gritty and annoying, or will I create more layers of pearl?

today I am...

a key

I hold the power to release the captive mind from its self-imposed prison. I've been here all along, forgotten in the shadowy recesses of shame. I've become rusty through many tears of regret, bitterness and sorrow.

I am the key and I am love. To open the lock I need to be turned twice. Once for acceptance; I accept whatever I said or did as a necessary part of my growth, no matter how foolish or selfish I might have been. The second turn is for forgiveness; I don't need to punish myself any more. Love is the key.

today I am...

a mandala

I am a mandala, a central point radiating outwards. My power lies in the centre — it is the source of all I am, and all I am capable of being.

The whole world is a mandala. From the solar system to an atom, the pattern of a central energy source surrounded by circles of energy is repeated endlessly.

Just like ripples on a lake, my thoughts and emotions permeate to the farthest reaches of my world, affecting each layer they pass through. Whenever I feel fragmented or spun out I bring my attention back to my centre, the source of my power.

today
I am...

I am

I am perfect as I am,
whatever I am.

100 WAYS TO MAKE YOUR LIFE
CALM AND CREATIVE

Today
I Will...

CARMEN WARRINGTON

**Do you want to live a life that is more calm,
more creative and more mindful –
but you're just not sure where to start?**

Today I Will… contains 100 affirmations
that will help you create the change you seek
in a simple, practical and joyful way.

You don't need to know how to meditate.
You don't need to have used affirmations before.
Just choose a page and be inspired
to start your new life … today.

Opening the door of your heart

And Other Buddhist Tales of Happiness

— • • • • — • • • • — • • • • —

AJAHN BRAHM

Modern tales of happiness, compassion and love that will both enlighten and entertain

Busy hours. Busy days. Busy lives. Obligations, relationships and worries.

This is daily life for so many of us. We know we need to slow down, to introduce mindfulness to our lives, maybe even to meditate. But how do we know where to start? To open the door of your heart is to take the first step. This collection of playful parables explores subjects such as hope, suffering, forgiveness, wisdom and unconditional love. They will make you laugh, move you and start you on your path.

These tales have been gathered over thirty years by Buddhist monk Ajahn Brahm, who lives in Australia; they have enlightened and inspired hundreds of thousands of readers worldwide.

WORLD-LEADING MEDITATION RESEARCH
FROM AUSTRALIA

RAMESH MANOCHA M.D.

SILENCE
YOUR
MIND

The scientifically proven approach
to meditation that will enhance
your wellbeing & performance –
in just 10 minutes a day

**Can't sleep because your thoughts won't
switch off?**

**Ever walked into a room to get something,
only to realise you've forgotten what you were
looking for?**

**Does a constant stream of chatter run through
your head?**

Silence Your Mind offers a ground-breaking approach
to meditation: the experience of mental silence. It clearly
explains how just 10 to 15 minutes of simple meditation
practice each day can turn off your unnecessary mental
chatter, thereby awakening your hidden abilities in work,
sport, studies and creative pursuits.

Australian Dr Ramesh Manocha is leading the world in
research into the positive impacts of the mental silence
experience. His findings show that authentic meditation
is easy, enjoyable, health giving and life changing.

Meditation can unleash your potential for good
mental and physical health and maximum performance,
and help you to live fully in the present moment.

If you would like to find out more about
Hachette Australia, our authors, upcoming events
and new releases you can visit our website,
Facebook or follow us on Twitter:

hachette.com.au
facebook.com/HachetteAustralia
twitter.com/HachetteAus

Carmen Warrington is a calm and creative author, actor, singer-songwriter, funeral celebrant and meditation artist living in Melbourne with her life partner and artistic collaborator David Jones. Together they create Soundbath Experience events (along with their singing bowls CD *The Hour of Nectar*), peace concerts, uplifting songs (Carmen crowdfunded her *Angel Songs* CD) and countless guided meditation recordings. Many have been made into YouTube videos and viewed over a million times. In 2010 ABC Music commissioned Carmen and David to create a series of eight CDs in the Meditations for Life series – the titles are *Peaceful*; *Take 5*; *Rest Well, Sleep Well*; *Relax*; *Worry-free*; *Healing*; *The Magical Forest* and *Today I Will…* which contains meditations inspired by her book of the same name.

For her latest audio releases please visit www.carmenwarrington.bandcamp.com and for news updates visit www.calmandcreative.com.au